LAST LOVE

FEELING ARE MORE POWERFUL THAN DREAMS SERIES - I

NAGASAI GANGINENI

I have my view of gratitude for my feelings and dreams that not more eventually to her...i really wished to have the person of the feeling i have .

The love is a word with a less enough of my feeling Ms.Bhavana .

Contents

Foreword   *vii*

Preface   *ix*

Acknowledgements   *xi*

Prologue   *xiii*

Last Love   *xv*

   1. S E R I E S - I 1st Day   1

   2. 2nd Day   3

   3. 3rd Day   5

   4. 4th Day   7

Word By The Author   9

Foreword

The book that i brought up here is all by a real incidents that took apart of mylife in my college life.

This is truly came up with my feelings that make me so distrubed on my way even all things around me are so negative ...i think the negativity is reason to read this you all

.

Preface

I remarked the Original preface to this book,it's easy to get sufficiently far away from it. The first sensations of finishing it , to refer it with the composure which this formal heading would seem to require. My interest in it was so recent and strong , and my was so divided between pleasure and regret-pleasure in the achivement of long design,regretin the seperation in many companions....,that i was in the danger of wearying thr reader with personal confidenc and private emotions .

Acknowledgements

I here being , within the hands of truth and my knowledge all the charecters , names and all therefore in the book are written in the consious state of mind .

Also the book invellets and the script are binded within my hands .

This include the conclude of Acknowledgement .

Prologue

I remarked the Original preface to this book,it's easy to get sufficiently far away from it. The first sensations of finishing it , to refer it with the composure which this formal heading would seem to require. My interest in it was so recent and strong , and my was so divided between pleasure and regret-pleasure in the achivement of long design,regretin the seperation in many companions....,that i was in the danger of wearying thr reader with personal confidenc and private emotions .

Last Love

" Last Love " is one the inspiring story i faced in the feeling of love .

It has been diveded in to two parts called " SERIES - I & II " .

CHAPTER ONE

S E R I E S - 1 1ST DAY

A boy of engineering final year , where he enjoys the life at his hands . In and out of the campus . The days are going so fast as his semister too....,A batch of 4 four are engaging in a classroom, where the class is going onn.....,putting the noise in the class with chit-chats and laughing allround commenting to the lectures in the classroom .

The day back from the college , the boy we are talking SAI came from college and rested up at the bed and scrolls up the mobile with a bottle of water with his routine night and he wakes up the new next day with the love hearted angry words by the mother . And he brushes up , dresses up and he starts the walks to his bus . Finally he gets in to his bus .

He has cameAfter the running of one hour , the bus enters into the college and finally SAI enter into the college and were roaming at each corner of class and enters into the first floor to second floor to the Department of Civil Engineering . And entered into the class where their are just half the strength of my branch with five of girls and twelve of boys after joining the first day of first class without my friends who used to meditate our names by our department of civil .

The time is runningup with moodoff in my first day even through our lectures are late to the class rooms that makes me the tough to handle the enjoyment and just roamed all over the campus . . . ,finally the day is ready to send us back to our homes . I wish that some colours(girls) to be fond at our beautiful place that everyday that we used to fun and flirt over colour(girls) is the place of resting up our buses to restdown our stress with the concept of love & flirtationship . . ,

.... day 1 @moodoff ....

I was waiting miserabily for the 'National Anthem' before time to leave i was sitting at back to the corner window of my left . . . . @nagasai344

CHAPTER TWO

2ND DAY

Wishing the day not to be the first day and i was started walking to the bus stop where all our college students gather for bus . . . finally i reached my bus stop thinking about the day ahead .

I feel the scene that i seen yesterday about love & flirtationship is usually a type of feeling like Happiness & Sadness , where the feeling in me of the feeling having undecidable thoughts in thinking (i was entered in the bus through the thinking of non-sense) .

The mood in the bus was good when compared yesterday . The colours(girls) are even likely unlike but the strength in bus is dominated by girls .

I was at the stop C , where the route of our bus is from (a-b-c-d-college) .

Finally we have reached the college . I was just stepped into the campus where i can hear the voice of our idiots . . . I was moving upstairs where i introduced myself to a new friend , i was carried my new friend into the voice our idiots(pranav , manikanta , poullesh , mohan) .

we have came up with the back of fun & commenting in corridors and stress downing by seeing colours(girls) . The classes are as normal as before with fun of backbenchers .

The time is up for buses .

I and my friends (pranav , mohan) were standing by the sitting wall beside of buses , all the colours are coming to our eyesight for their buses .

Even my eyesight is fallen on a girl that looks good in her mask , i was seeing her in silence . . . . . , and i lost her view of sight with blush of girls . . . . @nagasai344

2ND DAY - @FEELING

CHAPTER THREE

3RD DAY

The day yesterday is quite make me to go for college , where i were not seen a girl through and even i dont know name , class, branch, year, or anyelse i feel that something feeling like to see her again and again.....I was wakeup the day by the thoughts of her and I started walking for my bus .

I was sitting for my bus in my stop and my juniors are also came just a corner of me thinking about the girl who inspired of my feeling .

While thinking the bus was arrived and i boarded to my bus and seated in seat that near to the girls .

I was a student in my college where i get to flirt and enjoy the life in campus . I dont know about her that what make to think a lot .

Curving my charecter and attitude makes me happy for myself and the time the bus arrives the stop of her .....that i was seen while entering in the bus with a mask and her eyes are the magical app that make me to addict to her eyes . She came in to bus and sat in the 3rd seat of the bus in girls .

Seeing her eyes making me somthing that i never felt that i been with many of girls from my schooldays..this is a feel that i not able to tell by words .

I finally came in to the college , my friend mohan krishna called me to come to the water (one of a place that we all have fun) . I enterd in to the campus and met my friend mohn and i drank some water and my another friend pranav reddy also came their , we all make some fun together and time is up for our classes . The first period was running in my class and we are the three numbers me , pranav , manikanta who make the class in vibes and makes fun hard that we are also manages to study well not good so....like wise i make to go out in the break to search her with my friends without telling them and used search every class and i see twice the cass every time ....but even those their is no results in my searching ......

I got out of my campus after the time , where every one are comming out from the campus we three are waiting in the groud i was wishing and thinking that she will be come today i should talk at our bus......but she didnt come through the ground . I enterd to my bus and started cheaking for her with no results....while moving out the college at the gate of our collge the sirs and some students are enterd in bus even she came to bus from here.......i cannot see her even my environment is not good with full of students and standing along the bus ....and even sweating a lot .

Finally agin i seen her at her stop where she left up our bus..i feel ok . Thinking again that tommaro must be tell to her about all of this .

Even i came to the home with my unhappy face ...i dont know what me to find myself in her . I think that its charecter and atitude that brought up from her . i seen her in less seconds that make me think in hours to hours.....

......@nagasai344

CHAPTER FOUR

4TH DAY

I was getting time for my mid examination and the days are also going very fast . Today i were thinking that to talk to her in any of chances .As me thinking all those first i need to get ready for my college and i started getting ready and completed my breakfast and i started moving on my way to busstop .

All my juniors are are their before me . While i came within a minute of time our bus has arrived and i started boarding and seated as before . I was going in bus for a distnce and for sometime the stop of her has been reached .

I cheaked her she is in civil dress which looks good and beautyfull i fell that not to express and also not like a happy that is .

I seen her till she gets seated ; even every time i see she dosn't see me or anyone in bus she just dont know that even me is in the same bus . College has arrived i seen her she has dropped fast and moving to campus even i gets fast after i were losting her view ......,

Finally my friends mohan and pollesh came to me and started walking and even i told them about her i feel so lunlucky , the thing her i was joined the college and i proposed the girls with flirtationship and some of them are moved as i and some of them are said no .

I feel that all nothing more than flirt . but here is not same as that . I truly feel something about her and i romed all the rooms for her again as before day and the result is also same as yesterday , becaus ethe i dont know the name of her and anymore expect her village .

I dont know that what maks me up to feel .

Likewise i went my class after the break and its sports period for us . when all we are pranav , pollush , mohan krishna are going to buses on the way i seen her and told to them as she is the girl that makes me feel everyday and think off without no reason .

They are standing at the center of road to the canteen , where my friends are making sounds and shouting my name while crossing and went to canteen . And came back with nothing buying and aging while we are crossing them i seen her that she even seeing me. where she is not seeing me she looks casually about us . but the looks of her and my thoughts are mixed and make happy the day .

But i wished to speak to her . But i cannot .

....nagasai344

Word By The Author

@nagasai344

Feelings are just like a happy , sad and pain . The love is also a feeling that makes you fall all the feelings at a time .

We all know that anyone even cannot handle a single feeling as pain , sad or happy .

Feeling love is an toughest feel .

- NAGASAI GANGINENI .